Unswayed One Sail

101 LOVE SONNETS

Clyde A. Wray

editor: Deirdre R. Schwiesow
preface by Mike McDonell
introduction by the Poet Beth Anderson
cover photo "Beauty and Serenity" by Paula Stoeke
book design: Shelley Himmelstein

Poetry For Your Ear Publishing

Acknowledgement to Beth Brockman
Thanks for your belief

POEMS copyright @ 2000 by Clyde A. Wray

Poetry for Your Ear Publishing
e-mail: yourear@pacbell.net
web address: http://home.pacbell.net/yourear

All Rights Reserved
Printed in the United States of America
by Shalom Printing, Sherman Oaks, California
on Re:Vision kenaf/recycled paper/Soy ink.

Library Of Congress Catalog Card Number: 00-108575

ISBN 0-9659811-3-4

To Martha

Enjoy and read
only when in bed!
Be well

Clyde A. Wray
Feb 2, 2002

Preface

According to my Webster's, a sonnet is "a poem normally of fourteen lines in any of several rhyme schemes." This poor definition is hardly an adequate description of so pretty and, in the right hands, so powerful a poetic form. The Italian poet Giovanni Petrarcca (Petrarch) set the stage for the sonnet's enduring popularity during the Italian Renaissance and undoubtedly influenced it's English master, William Shakespeare, two hundred years later. Today, poets still use the sonnet to give their thoughts and emotions form. Why? For the same reason that we exercise any traditional discipline: for the parameters that allow us to soar, to rise above.

Clyde A. Wray is a friend and uncommon poet who has been soaring since I first met him almost ten years ago. He is a friend who has helped many in many different ways and an "uncommon poet" because the creation of poetry is his vocation, not his hobby. And he is very good at what he does. With this collection of sonnets (101), Wray's output approaches the Bard's (154); but it is the subject (love) not the quantity of sonnets which occupies both poets. It is the quality of verse that is the measure of the poet and the sonnet maker. Shakespeare's place is set. Within this volume, another poet takes risks and seeks to take us higher than we ever could imagine on words of love, words that make us soar and yearn for more. Enjoy the trip and ride with Clyde A. Wray, a master poet and "love-soarer."

Mike McDonell,
Co-founder of The Memorial Day Writers' Project and Instructor of Creative Writing at Northern Virginia Community College

Introduction

Several years ago Clyde A. Wray gave his first poetry reading in
Portrait of a Bookstore's patio garden. We had been honored by
his presence among the other writers who come to our bookstore
café to work and had come to think of him as our poet in
residence, seated at his table pursuing his poetic vision with
remarkable focus and intensity. To hear him perform his work
then, lifting the word up off the page in the embrace of his
beautiful voice, I was spellbound. Cast a spell he did, as all true
poets must.

The authenticity of Clyde's call to the poet's work is beyond
question. I have always admired the unwavering commitment he
has made to his work, or rather his poet's life because certainly
there is no longer any distinction between the two. Clyde is part
of that ancient lineage of wandering truth-tellers, bards, prophets
and troubadours, unfettered by our ordinary accumulation of
possessions and expectations, notions of the good life at odds
with our deepest sense of ourselves. It is his gift, from the depth
of his personal history, his wide-ranging travels, his fundamental
poetic freedom, to offer us in his poetry an insistent,
compassionate vision of our humanity, person
by person.

I was not surprised when Clyde turned to sonnet form, taking
as his subject love and its eternal longings, raptures and losses,
always reflective, always engraving itself into our physical
memory. His poetry had always been both the search for
connection and an immersion in memory. This search for

understanding of our disparate impulses we depend upon a poet of his skill to reconcile. Yet I was not prepared for the depth with which he engaged this form so steeped in the echoes of long tradition. His appropriation of the form, its cadences and language, turning them to his own purposes is audacious. Even while being swept along in the precision of his passionate renderings of love's many faces, I found myself laughing out loud at his verve, the sweep of his language, his courage. One poet's appreciation of another's high-wire act.

Yet it takes no special knowledge in the craft of poetry to answer the heart of these poems. Often, as here, the greater poetic skill is in the disappearance of form itself into the poem's immediacy. Clyde A. Wray has infused the sonnet with the power and play of his language, the gift of his steady gaze on our human condition. Anyone can hear this poet's voice calling us to listen and delight. I invite you to do so.

Beth Anderson
Poet

That mine eye should light upon thy face is not mere
happenstance—
fates being constant and their motions decreed,
where'er my maiden steps, there I should be.
Yet methinks no painter of portraits in fine oils, water,
acrylics can capture the light streaking through thy hair
nor temperament or skin tone that puts others to pale.
No painter's brush or canvas can attest the most beauteous
of mine eye, hence, many think I lie. Yet noble, sound of heart
and truth, forever I declare: there is no fairer maiden
I pine for throughout the year. Therefore, my lady in the forest,
where'er thy steps take you, there I should be; but should
I tarry, 'tis but out of fear that once escorted through the wood,
upon these ears the sweet bird voice of yours to hear:
"From this point I travel on, but lo, I go alone."

Sonnet 2

When fleeting time remarks, "He was other than a poet,"
and thy love for me has passed (for time itself will change; its
sorrow passes with each changing moon, joy arises with the sun),
speak of me: of boisterous voice, of passion grand, loving life
and the land, with words that jump the sun, of having thrown my
kisses after the seasons, of gall and guile, having ridden clouds,
perhaps a pinch of mirth and an inch of worth.
Say: "Many offense did he commit, a traveler wide and far, to his
honor he held hard, like reins to a shooting star. Alas, like the
star he flamed out, having gone the charted course. We'll see his
like no more, liberty assured like the coming of the ocean tide
or the blueing of a gray sky." But, before this unfolding,
the more 'tis now I'll say to you clearly,
I'd never a cheap thought of you, and I love you deep and dearly.

Dark the plot against me in the witching hour, to lure me by stealth, unseen design, from the dwelling place within thy heart, thus to rob me of your light. For in the eye of my detractors, fair is fair, love's war games lend no relief. The art of war is knowing, and know they there are miles between hearts in which to skirmish. Thus they spoil my reputation, heap upon me humiliation, for they know at this distance there is no defense; but truth will have its final say, pulled from the scabbard of righteousness as a scythe to cut across a field of wheat. There in the bright light of day will I be exonerated, thus bide them care—war knows no lack of guilt in idle gossip, nor cares much who swims the mire or offends. So, thank you for thy passion's fire, not influenced by others' nefarious desires. May the muse forever smile down at you, pleased.

Sonnet 4

O, from whence doth come this eternal flame burning in my
breast,
that lays not down, giveth no peace, allows not the mind to rest?
How this meteoric rise, fevering my very brow, a yearning so
intense, in competition with the sun, burns the very grass that I
tread upon? Where then is the cooling wind to temper the
unskilled heart, that which with unkind word like dazzling
crystal splinters into a million parts? That the fates should cast
such a blow I dare not believe, though my beloved knows not of
my existence, fear grips at my throat when I dare to speak, to
gaze upon her countenance saps my strength, turns me docile,
meek.
How then will she look to me, as I traverse among her peers,
imploding? From those outside myself I seek relief—
to poets whose songs and sonnets that through the ages
turned heads of many a fair lady, I plead.

O, how can I in contemporary kind woo thee? Thy mind is set in modern living and I, dreaming of Elizabethan days—of quills, flattery, and romance that befits thee.

Dull has my existence been, but oh, 'tis with faith in knowing this separation's not set in permanence. Mine eye has not seen clearly, nor a day gone by painless, for 'tis pain not to have you near me (though each day is a day of beauty—to think otherwise is ungodly—nevertheless, I've wept). Aye, never to be sorry for love's tyranny, nor will conceit please thee, but I praise the passing of the winter, rejoice in the coming of the spring. For in an hour darkly, wings of a bird bring thee to me, but betwixt now and then, my life's composition shall know melancholy as a friend.

Yet, when I sleep you will be near me, time will be a supporter: I will have shown no motion, the interval will have shrunk.

Sonnet 6

Not being fleet afoot nor having wings to soar
awkward with my pen no poetry that roars
no mastery of art, stone, or masonry
in a world of color these brown eyes see gray
no player of the lute, lyre, or angelic harp
music is foreign and a world apart
eyes that cloud over in the world of art
still richly blessed to know beauty above the rest
she's flawless and magnificent, full of worldly zest
she's light in a world dark with hatred
a song to be sung soft and light-tempered
like a soft cool wind blowing gently unrestricted
Though art and music are unknown to me
art and music she must be.

Now must men concur, as brother to brother, that to each there is but one lady that resides in his heart beyond all others. To each comes a rosebush, with prickly pricks and thorns, that each to a man would mourn, if in the morning found it gone. Therefore, shallow pride I cast aside, take pen in hand, lavish upon you words old and new, and those of a penitent. For my love for you is boundless, has no charted course, like a timeless wave has no restrictions, blows with a gale's force. What was a trifling life is now dignified—you've put the majesty in the day. For deeds not yet done and those that passed, if some have caused you pain, here and now I take this vow as sure as the sun is dawning: May the gods look upon me unfavorably, give not a hint of warning. For fragile is my Rose; she makes my garden, surely I would mourn, if in the morning I awoke, and found my lovely gone.

Sonnet 8

O, if the tales historians tell of William Shakespeare's
sonnets carry a grain of truth, I know to the marrow what he felt
when he wrote them: of the nights and days, the hellish storms,
the power of love and its many forms—its moods and doubts,
                                                        heavy
black clouds, the acid tears when s/he wasn't around. I know why
he wrote and wrote. I know the silver lake where her reflection
was born, of the poetry in her song, to be struck by a form of
lightning which is the power of love. I know of his solitary
days and confinement, his state of mind, why he floated when he
walked, the reasons for the broad grin when he talked.
I know the virtue of his pen; I know why there's no variation
or quick change in his sonnets. As he said to her, I say to you:
       "For as the sun is daily new and old,
         so is my love still telling what is told."*

*William Shakespeare, Sonnet #76

So doth my soul cry out this night, being struck dumb;
no words from this poet's mind have yet spoken to my
lover's heart. For my love's beauty impairs my sight—
sightless I stumble through the night (the night being the
working hour, I'm rendered forlorn, at loss of word power).
Yet the stars do glitter, ah, there's a ray of hope,
a flicker of a word coming within my scope, four letters
not to be abused. With each sight of her it's fanned anew,
for she is love, and loves light, gently sleeping through the
night, and I with unworthy pen invent and note each graceful
purring breath. Has there ever been a man such as I, so blessed
(once fraught with rude crudeness) to have such a beautiful muse?
Whilst I call for her aid in this hour darkly, alone, I know I'm
so richly blessed, to be a witness while she's at rest.

Sonnet 10

Know not I if she's fond of praise, or of, to her, the words I've
                                                              writ,
or of my tortured soul which she knows not she holds captive.
'tis true, very true, I walk on trembled legs, at a glance of her
or the breath of her name; shamed I'm not, bearing the torch
flaming within my breast. I hold it high, my banner, my coat of
arms, no prouder man than I. She's no mere trophy, she's the air
I need to exist, she's the jewel in the eye of every man.
Would that she'd cast an eye to me; know not I if she's proud of
a single word I've writ, but if fortune smiles, tomorrow comes, I've
the will to try again. A slave am I to my ageing heart, her youth
bears only joy, and time will have its way with me—indifferently
the clock continues on.
Antiquity do your best, parchment yellow, decay, but
the words of praise I write to her shall never ever fade.

Foolish men with lascivious heart
wild of eye know nothing modest
do plunder and spoil lack taste and never toil
braggarts each and flowers they despoil
liars, black-hearted, and vile and beyond repair
do foul and pollute the air
boisterous and dense of heart
not loving themselves, beauty, or art
loathsome they wander the night
to play in what's ugly, shallow, and blight
the devil's their own, angels take flight
seeking safer passage throughout the night;
God watches over his angels in flight
gives safe harbor both day and night.

Foul, he that called me friend quietly
sued thy love away from me mockingly
cut the ties that bound us permanently
surely as the seas pound the shore heavily
yet even in this hour darkly
my love goes on unceasingly
through the woe but knowingly
the dark comes before the dawn angrily
dawn's light comes brightly, serenely
and he that covets will be rewarded justly
the pain which is mine presently
surely will be his alone hopefully;
And even through the fire of my tears
my love will settle like dew to linger on many years.

She has no shame—laying in her lair, with tawny skin, coal black wiry hair, panther-black eyes piercing through the enclosed balcony air, feline sleek. She's the type of woman men dream to meet: dangerous, daring, above others' reproach; she'd cast you aside with the bat of one panther's eye. Icy steel and concrete her domain, a jungle of nameless faces wandering, etched with pain. She watches these creatures far below her lair, a bemusing thought—could there be a partner out there? A critical thinker, agile, swift, he'd hold his own, he'd be the pride of the pride, judicious, above hate. Night has begun far below, a single stream of headlights moving to and fro, streets damp from an early rain, faceless men, women, gone to shelter with their pain.
Now is her time to devour life, with stealth and intrigue, moving with grace on the sharp edge of night.

Sonnet 14

(To A Father Suffering The Loss Of A Daughter)

Mine eye sees the sadness, depth of pain in your soul, of a
father's love for a daughter beyond reach, beyond control. O
wretched heart, what pain she must have borne to give up the sun,
wilt beneath the bluest skies, share stars with you no more. A
father's love by standard goes perilous as ship to tempestuous
sea, or smooth as a moonlight cruise sailing the Aegean Sea.
But lo the darkest night is on you, a night your mind could
never invent, a night so dark it saps you of strength and breath.
Your daughter heard the wailing, heard Hydra's call on starless
night in the grayest hours before dawn; broken-hearted you
couldn't divine her agony or distress, or feel a light will e'er
shine within your breast again.
Though you're wounded gravely, cut down to the quick, know as
father of a daughter, I most profoundly share your woe.

Sonnet 15

Justice will find its light of day
and I my month of May
for I surmised better that he have her
than I come to bitter
better I stop trying
stop look to dying
come out straightaway
to the light to roses to gay
to life's mystery of what's in store for me
roads to travel and mystic beings
all things that flourish in the light of day
till once again will come my May;
Justice will come one day
certainly to my May.

Sonnet 16

O, that she cast an eye to me
she the most beauteous by far
on lands across the bountiful seas
she kindles the fires within my breast
makes a furnace of my soul
quenches not my thirst for her
yet she I cannot hold
she that knowest only fair for fair
no lip to lie of chaste heart
she holds another dear
so pine I in quiet solitude
and dark confinement alone;
She being out of reach
turn I inward for myself to sleep.

Tis not for nothing a wretch such as I:
yowl at the sky, blaspheme the night
scrutinize craters of the moon and the
constellations for a Venus—for this earth-born
mortal is barren, no love cometh in any season.
Know not I why or reason; she has seized
my heart, then fled, leaving in her wake false
the air with platitudes, saying: A good man I
but better she found to stand in my stead.
Thus, she being false to me, my sorrow grows
without consent, the die's been cast,
and I all spent. Yet!
Pride shall rise on the morrow, perfumed and in repair—
death to sorrow; welcome will be fresh morning air.

When all others have been prophet of my cause
and I speechless within thy sight (as stars vanish in
daylight as opposed to night), lest you wonder at
my lack of conviction, you are the poetry that brings
life to this wretched pen. That I might have just
cause in such an unworthy state, ponder I:
how to tempt an angel to favor me, dote on me,
dwell not on my insufficiency or
have cause to hate, but to affirm the wretchedness
of my fate. Therefore my love story goes untold
hearing the sweet nightingale sing, perchance
you think me a fool, thus I say this:
A fool I may seem, but you I carry within
my heart, mind; you are the sweetest of dreams.

When time comes that we by night or day
be parted, and in the night comes the capricious thief
by stealth to take love away—whether it's from you or me
(for he is arbitrary, he gives no time, rhyme, or reason
he travels far, arrives in any season)
you or I should stay not long with injury or sorrow
should acquaint oneself again with life on the morrow
mourn not long for a sweet deceased
think they lie in the state of grace
that they live in the bosom of a happy place.
The knock shall come for one and all
and all will leave, be it in winter, spring, summer, or fall;
If it be me and twice in heaven there happiness be
then twice I would have married thee.

Sonnet 20

Sweet thy dreams be, my love, for as you slumber
night is perfumed by the freshness of thy hair,
of lilacs and rosewood placed by you near.
For this be the hour of my advantage, when I compile
and chronicle the virtue of thy deeds.
Methinks to trumpet to the world o'er distant shores
the purity of thy soul: how you toiled o'er adversity
to claim many victories ever most graciously, for
this is a beholder you've robbed of all uncertainties.
As thou dost make my nights day and my days bright,
I must proclaim, report, the beauty of thy soul.
So sublime a love you give, it makes this heart whole.
Slumber, slumber well, for in your slumber there is peace;
whilst you slumber shall I erect in words another monument.

Sonnet 21

Has my world, in which your beauty lives, set its course
to an implosion? When my life appears out of sorts and I forlorn
and in distress, first must I look to my own impediments:
To my own cruel and imperfect tongue, and where it has laid
disgrace and shame, naught but my own self to blame, lest
I lay my woe to others before I make my own plague right
(for I've been not holy nor virtuous when the day turned into
night).
Thus I invoke the muse, to remove this brooding, to give me
contentment of its choosing. But if it would ask of me what this
contentment be, my tongue will speak of thee: as fortune found
in the early morn, to keep your love from dusk till dawn
and never forsake or bear that love a wrong.
As you are the greatest treasure sent down from the heavens,
methinks to look upon you will always bring contentment.

Sonnet 22

Let's forget about the morrow
today let us watch the daisies grow
leave behind the sorrow
scream no to the world of woe
let us joy in this early morn
put our bright in the dawn
squeeze the love of nature
in our every song
come back you lie down beside me
you're my poetry and my prayer
where ever you choose to step
my love for you is there;
forgotten about the morrow there is no more woe
your smile in morning touches the very depths of my soul

Sonnet 23

When comes my angel to shine her light on me,
to caress me on her bosom close, as if to give sanctuary,
to give me the wisdom of her way (albeit I falter
from dawn to the closing of the day)—where then
is my love? Not ill-mannered but gifted in harmony,
with the sun so much that she'd bring glory to the day;
yes! when comes my love to shower me with kisses
so I mayn't stray, to lie with me in the depths of night
to keep my fears at bay? O would that she were here
in this hour of evening's glow. But no... So walk I
beneath a heavy cloud, head bowed in the shadow
of sorrow, sorrow a friend I've come to know.
Yet, whilst these eyes can see into a dream, surely
in a dream of this scope there's always that eternal hope.

Twas but once I laid mine eyes on thee; swift
as an arrow felt I the full weight of spring.
With it came wondrous, delightful imaginings
of things that come when one walks in a dream:
velvet blue flowers, cinnamon-colored skies, love
that envelopes you, never a tear to dampen the eye,
undying gratitude for an angelic smile,
a certainty that for thy love I would die. But lo,
knows well my heart what is—a dream is for dreaming's
sake; not for reality does dreaming make. Thus
this sweet discontent and ill-gotten fever
blows with a passion's fire the desire to be near her.
Vainly I return to the place where first I discerned her,
my Rose. Unsatisfied I fled; now I see her everywhere.

Whene'er I've noticed my heart is least full
and sadness covers my eyes
turn I inward, ponder the question why.
How and why this pain, remorse? Could it be for love
long ago lost? Could it be all else pales against all reason,
my desire for her not yet out of season?
Or is such the weakness I've attained, that none other
can favor gain? How long this woeful debate,
how long the intention to attend this state?
Better served I'd be to acquaint myself with loss and grief,
for like the wild bird once set on the wing, she'll never
return to me, for in her freedom there contentment be.
Therefore, if in freedom there happiness be
then it's my own self I must set free.

Sonnet 26

Dear wife—these words ring true
that begin this sonnet I write for you
not the mere imaginings
of one who travels reckless through a dream;
I'm not often given to flowery speech
or known to say that which can be impeached
yet you are the color that lights my dawn
your spirit gives the wind its song
to watch inflamed fires in your cheeks turns sunrise meek
always about you a fragrance sweet
who about you has a fairer glow? surely there be none I know
you've been kissed by the dove of love
Cherubs circle on high—young, fair, pure, heavenly sweet—
betwixt you and they, happy the comparisons greet.

Sonnet 27

On the shore dreaming, which oft I'm wont to do
there beneath the azure sky oft I dream of you.
And there comes but one unsure thought: if of me
you have cared ought, if in some pleasant way
a kind thought of me this day.
Surely on this day of spring
a word, keepsake, or cherished remembering of me.
But I digress, for I hold what heaven has blessed
placed firmly in a locket, deep within my pocket,
a lock of your yellow tresses to caress at my pleasure.
This little that heaven has sent me, I'll take gladly, freely—
a momentous occasion to hold it to my heart dearly.
I hold your imprisoned hair, yet never beyond my scope—
it is your passion and love for which I so dearly hope.

Sonnet 28

Aye, what's this pounding of the drum?
Tis my heart being overcome
know I why this void—the width of its scope
perplexing this feeling, this lack of hope
this blinding light of being taken unaware and by surprise
this searing burning in my brain;
it's thoughts of her brings this pain.
Yet I dream of slamming doors, 'tis
fear of seeing her no more. Nor can I hear
others speak, her voice alone though deep I sleep
from whence came my soul to this fire
why night so long? Alas, 'tis her passion song I so desire;
why, within me this fire burning deep
'tis the passion for her love and light which I keep.

Sonnet 29

Nay friend, sleep is no friend to me
for in my sleep her portrait I see
and hear the echo of her call, see her gliding
elegantly, softly down the hall. No friend,
sleep is no friend of mine or refuge to find peace,
there her music and slender fingers on the keys,
no not in sleep is there ease; awake find I a better
distraction, all about me night-life's action:
the thunder of a waterfall, nightbirds' mating call
an astronomer I, watching stars traverse across the universe
perhaps with a cat's eye glimpse my former love
feasting, dancing through the night.
Yet, the sun brings no ray of hope of how to cope, no cheer
in the light of day heart throbbing, what's this in my eye?

a tear.

Sonnet 30

Surely as does the night turn into day
is as often as I've lost my way; yet always
in pursuit of truth, it is part of my roots
as roots are grounded in mother earth. Where,
I ask, is my authenticity—that which makes me, me?
I not born of nobility, and lacking in gentility.
Truth's like a cold cup of gruel; yet cruel though it may be
the aftertaste leads to a fresh-water stream to wash
the foulness away. Aye, the journey is unending, each dawn
a new day, and He that made us has the last say.
Look I forward to the morrow—its joys, its sorrows;
His hand to lead the way, in the hard light of truth I'll stay.
For this journey to the truth I'd no patience in my youth;
O what antiquity can do, and He above sent me you.

These clouds of doubt that come with winter scene
lay overcast on my being. Their blinding torrents take control,
icy fingers down my spine that hold me, as in a whiteout
blind me. O these uncertainties, from whence do they
come to me to conjure up such strange imaginings,
creating havoc in my brain? It's the midnight hour;
you're wrapped up warm in your sleep.
I despise the thoughts I keep but my love
for you runs deep. Winter seems an eternity, beg I much
for the light of spring, you and I in a wooded glen,
kissing you Kellyn in my garden, and I not so weather-beaten,
all doubts would be suspended.
Welcome it will be when you awake, for you are spring—
where you walk and talk, the sun shines and everything is
                                                   uplifting.

Closes his eye so's not to see what befell him uncomfortably.
Picks up devil's brew, numbs his mind, sees not the truth:
how she beguiled him with her charming way whilst
he lavished on her praise from dusk to day. Poor fool—
cunningly she did wound him and at night betrayed
she the dawn of love that filled his soul. When he was unloved
she made him whole; now this love has sealed his fate.
She he won't debase, for love says act not in haste.
Therefore, a forfeiture of gentle dreams and peace.
for with every kiss there is a lie, with it a piece
of him dies from love or conceit, but with eye closed
he comes not to know his self-deceit.
Yet, even with these words writ of her this day
'tis with love, and hope she'll come home to stay.

'Tis bittersweet, it is, to have loved and lost
the price of losing high the cost,
the loss of your kiss leaves empty every room
thus travel I the roads in the state of perpetual gloom:
this endless procession of words, this bleeding heart,
hours spent longing for a love that will return not,
shadows on the walls that walk in despair
no glimmer of light or hopes of repair,
weeds in the garden black like a tomb and I
outside your window under a blue-gray moon
to glimpse a sight of you in the damp chill air, your
reflection gracing the window, is time spent well there.
Aye, and each day I'm given a voice to speech
is each day always in praise of your love I'll preach.

Sonnet 34

Why this night so dark and I so filled with dread?
Why up, and not in bed? Why this sadness which
envelopes me when I look down, lay my eye on thee?
O, these insecurities from past relationship—
wild, open, and free—chill my blood with fear
of you leaving me. Thou art the calm to my storm,
my summer breeze that keeps me warm,
a gale-force wind when I am wrong,
your name is whispered in my every song.
Your hand I touch while you sleep; pure dread
overcomes me, for my love for you runs deep, deeper
than the bluest of seas, deeper than you'll ever see.
Such is my love for thee it steals my sleep,
while not sleeping I pray to Him your love to keep.

Sonnet 35

Know I the warmth of the hollow of your neck,
the satin sheen of your skin, the length
of your fingers as they curl around my hand.
But more, know I where the golden heart is stored,
where is kept the flaming lamp to bring the light
into your eye, know I the secret pain you hide,
of all the wealth of dreams gone unsatisfied.
Yet methinks you're heaven's best
as gods have told it, their invention
above all the rest—in you they find no fault.
So rare a bird you are in flight, flying with the doves;
make a request, what you ask shall be yours.
If more love without condition or contrition is your desire,
the gods and I shall conspire to give you more of what you
require.

Sonnet 36

Why should love bring on such weeping
a cracked heart, open bleeding
that a man in such disrepair loves a woman
beyond all hope? O the agony and the woe
none to tell and none may know
lest they think him base and grave
that he idles his days away; know not they
of how she affected him, a teasing kiss—all went dim.
Without her love all is dark, dank, and grim
she is Muse, air, light, and such a gentle breeze
a face that keeps angels transfixed and pleased.
She is etched within his heart, silently he grieves;
Great and little men may do manly things
for the love of a woman go they into the night
                                        whimpering.

Sonnet 37

Seeking fourteen lines of starlight
fourteen lines of beauty that might light
upon your ear fourteen lines to bring you near
fourteen lines of wonder for you to hear;
fourteen lines you haven't heard before
fourteen lines and not a line more
fourteen lines to seal within your breast
fourteen lines to kiss you like angels breath
fourteen lines to melt the shell around your heart
fourteen lines from you which will never depart
seeking fourteen lines of starlight
fourteen lines to capture from this very night;
All fourteen lines captured are you
full of wonder moonlight all true.

Sonnet 38

Naught but the elements to slow my steed
to distant lands with haste and speed
from sheriff in gallant pursuit with none
but the thought of knot and noose. As I
speed through wooded glen my regrets around
me fall, that I shan't see thy smile at all
or taste thy lips more succulent than a honeycomb
nor ever again hear the echo of thy call. O
much reason I've given thee just cause to hate
for when I slew him I set my fate
setting my desire before all good thought
in pitch of night, untethered anger injustice brought.
Though sheriff's eyes speak fair, they are of ice—
methinks perhaps he thinks of how to hang me twice.

Unswayed she came as if by perfumed cloud
such is the beauty of my Rose, for her skin
as fair as any petals, a face as soft, sweet
disarms all who come to greet her; her
enchanting beauty beyond all comparisons meet
and I with gluttonous desire woo her in night's cover
covet her, drowning in my passion's heat: yearly
and in every season, that I much love her
in my fashion but goes unspoken, blushing unreasoning;
thus I call upon my Muse to give me a poet's tongue
to heap praise from these lips give them songs to be sung
gods I ask, let her lend an ear to a poor untutored song;
And yet, she is of the world, skilled and fair
Methinks I've naught to offer and naught to compare.

Sonnet 40

Aye, how much more of the splendor of the sun
can shine in her eyes, the freshness of a pure lake
be on her lips, the rose's color be in her cheeks
or the voices of angels heard when she speaks?
What is more pleasurable than to watch her sleep?
She's my soul's desire; she alone my heart wants and keeps;
lucky I am friend to thee I can impart these thoughts
but in truth, from thee envy it brought;
like the crier into the wind you loudly declared me unfit
unbeknownst to me, she you've much longed to be with;
gravely dear friend had I known of your woe
forever these things would have gone untold.
Friend, forthwith I shall censure my tongue
but know that I and she will forever be one.

There be no night longer than this:
endless, unyielding, darker than the deepest sea.
Nowhere, close or far, do I feel thy presence about me.
Pray then, where art thou, my love? Hast thou
forgotten that hearts entwined are hearts never lost,
but the absence of one leaves the other to pay the cost?
O this woe-begotten soul without thee aimlessly roams
with judgement impeded, goes port to ports unknown,
with foul mood and uncaring tongue lashing out
at friend and foe in the early morn till the sun doth go.
Wretched me, I find no pleasure in ports of call where
others leisure; search I to find my golden treasure.
Yet, near or far my heart doth bleed—
as the choice is hers, she stays beyond my reach.

Whilst thee mayn't anymore as suitor
acknowledge me, be swift,
eye to eye say we canst ever be;
Then mine heart
will take its flight to heal, mend
perchance to comprehend the tragic end
of how it came to suffer its double loss
of Muse and lover; of how our stars passed, crossed
of how we burst and flamed across the sky
for others to witness and marvel as flew we by
then on a muddy day with whispered breath
clouds poured rain, the dream of love washed away.
Though double the pain plus twice the loss
happy the minutes were, though high the cost.

Sonnet 43

Tell, what's this jewel that cavorts across the sky,
that dares to be bold, to place sparkles in my darling's eye?
In boldness its glowing rays sprout the seeds
of love and kindness, food of human need.
It casts away tomb-like gloom with great aplomb,
spreads its warmth and joy—it touches everyone.
Why so kind as it sits so high in the air? Aye,
perhaps looking down it senses some despair
and at night it mustn't tarry, it must go in, it
cares enough to send out thousands of its friends
to brighten the landscape, they dart in and out; to
make love in their light is a poetic end of a night.
Let the jewels forever cavort across the sky—
blessed a man I am to see them dancing in my darling's eye.

Alas, 'tis besieged, this weary brain,
laid low by anger and disdain.
Methinks Providence has turned its back to me
by that act snatched my light away from me.
How am I to find glory in His day
when He doth inflict such brutal pain?
Find I no just cause, for from my heart
methinks I gave her all. This night I bear Him ill,
for with her my cup was much filled.
But lo, He hath given—he may take away;
on this night methinks not to bend a knee to pray
and thereby give glory to this ill-fated day.
Blessed be the Father and the Son
though I blaspheme, pray I, bring back my love.

Sonnet 45

If ever again mine eye should see
such a one most beauteous as thee
no other near or far shall ever fulfill my need.
Whene'er I heard thy poetic call
it came to my ear as an angel's song;
whene'er thy hand was placed in mine
the warmth of it caused the sun to shame, to hide
and I secured to thee as a clinging vine to tree—
in the shade of your love I'm made complete.
O that I could reach up and place before your eye
a bouquet of stars so thou shouldn't be denied
the wonders of the heavens as clouds roam by.
I've naught to give and less to share but by your leave
I'll struggle long, hard, to get a rainbow for your hair.

If in the telling there be truth then speak,
aye speak, be not of held tongue
truth is in need of light and I'm in need of some.
Be like the cathedral bell loudly rung, then I shan't dwell
where broken hearts live in the unknowing hell;
speak, though like rushing rivers tears will flow
if to be locked away from heaven, least I'll know
speak in an unguarded way will it be the morrow
or shall the gates close today beginning my sorrow?
for I am undone and loose at the edges
oppressed with pain at the loss of privilege
speak with honor then there'll be no sacrilege.
But lo, speak with tempered tongue
the loss of love leaves one to mourn long.

Once with thee my heart was lifted up
being pleased to labor for labor of love.
But with thy charm thou hast made sport
of my devotion, and you were in a shadow plot.
Thy deception was artfully done, beguiling subtleties—
therein lies the deepest cut and vilest of cruelties.
Like to a masterpiece, thou hast made a forgery
of love's art, and I with false artistic eye,
bartered and spent, much enthralled 'came
ruefully aware I had that which was counterfeit.
Canst there be a more heinous crime committed
or deed so foul than to be betrayed by one false-hearted?
Yet whilst I look upon your portrait true
there be no sign of falseness in you.

Though we two of strange alchemy
in the sight of others out of step, but free
give time its best as time requires
love its glory—it's God-inspired. With each
passing of a September's moon this man's report
no greater debt will he ever beget nor pray, abort;
glory to that Indian summer His work of art
a place of honor within this man's heart
to have reaped from you a magnificent harvest
a full measure of love, to forever digest;
never again to suffer the woe, the emptiness
nor the poorness of spirit and soul—
The joy of you has enriched my palate; inundated
with your richness this man is much sated.

It came clearly in a midnight dream
a rush of wind, the chill of my impending doom
the hour the day our paths would part
icy words would split my heart; O
in the shadow of a moon's eerie glow
before me you stood, then with haste withdrew,
there in your eye not deceit but truth
age is an impediment to your youth.
As winter is to spring briefly did a heart sing
quick like the leaves of autumn our love went falling
scattered on old gray benches where an old man came to rest
remembering lively days, younger and at his limberest;
O to have foreseen such, in such a torturous dream
evaporates what's left of life's years, dries them up like steam.

Sonnet 50

Provocateurs, rhymers, sound loud their report
singers sing their songs of thy amorous ways—
bereft, jealous, for none have had their day
to lie with thee in golden fields of sunflowers and hay
nor speak of conquest or say they had their way.
For thou art Nature's truth thus rising above reproof.
Aye, jealousy has no shame in its anguish, its pain
cares not where it leaves its blackest lie or darkest stain.
Therefore, once a day, for countless days and two score,
this voice will create thy legend of honor, others to be ignored.
As the royal guardsmen man the gates, I to your honor
'till my dying breath shall attest that where you stand is hallowed.
Just as the oceans since forever just seem to be,
so will my love forever just be for thee.

If my love for thee has no purpose
why then do I so maddeningly possess it?
If my love for thee has no purpose
why this fire of desire for consummation of it?
O, that I could place before your eye this branded
soul bewitched by thee, that by bewitching me, you control.
O love runs unabated, you want not what you've created.
On me thou hast marked thy name, brought me low,
an illness of shame where this fire burns, but stagnated.
I have sworn none other shall light mine eye
if not the love of thee, then a life with love I'll be denied—
shall thee to me in error prove, of illness I'll soon be cured.
The stars of the universe of which I've no control,
the fire given freely is from a mind, body, and soul!

And yet there's no sunrise without you
No purpose without your song
No harmony in the scheme of things
No warmth in a house that's bare
No twinkle in the sky above
just the emptiness of space
No perfume wafting through the air
No sense of time or place
No jasmine in the garden
only the barrenness of soil
No reminder of the glow of love
of which once you gave your all.
And death is the keeper, the keeper of your flame
hasten I to go there, unencumbered, unashamed.

Sonnet 53

Unyielding, stalking into the depth of night
clearly never far from sight
seeking to bend and break the will
sap the strength, erode the skill.
Cast shades of doubt, increase the fear
behind the back steal one that's dear
and with cowardly innovation
let some linger, suffer from your intention
and with blatant lie
lead some to believe you have a brighter side.
But those sitting in the eye of grief
know you to be a darkly-cloaked thief;
what you've snatched up and stolen away
leaves tears in a heart and a fragmented day.

I'll sue the heavens and the earth
sue the gods for every cent you're worth—
demand that they give up their spoils
stand them up, put them out on the dole
snatch the sun from their eyes
then watch the gods cry, and
fumble about the galaxy.
May the gods be damned, cursed
to blindly roam their universe.
What they could have, they chose not to avert—
they laid me low with the most grievous hurt
removed the star from my eye, worse...watched her die.
May the heavens be made to crumble at my feet—
never again will the world know one so gentle, so sweet!

If you be near to me
nearer still, closer come to me
whisper comfort and gentle be
let the warmth of thy body cover me
splay these hands upon thy body fair
these fingers comb the abundance of thy hair
lead me to where heaven waits
where our love merges and bliss is our fate
a storm about us shall we create
in a field of stars under lavender sky
we pledge love one thousand times amplified
'till one or the other or both have died.
Let the world be mad, untethered, frayed—
our passion for life and love is inviolate, unafraid.

Sonnet 56

Though thou mayest think I do abandon thee
never my love think that it could be
as light never truly abandons the sky
never shall it pass thou art far from my
inner eye. But destiny laid this field to plow
wanting or not, go I must for now
with the weight of thee within my breast
thy warmth and scent upon my chest;
I find no grace in the eye of middle age
where fear abounds, life unwinds, disengages.
But keep me in the shelter of thy memory,
kind thoughts, and in thy dreams I'll be;
And when I walk corridors of darkened halls
I'll remember thee bright as that candle flame of love.

Sonnet 57

In the shelter of the glow of love, out of the rain
love locked in our hearts, sitting under a Joshua tree
speak of love, you and me, plans we make to carry through
promise to smell the freshness of the morning dew
to wake to love, not despair, to walk long roads though they be
                                                              hard
a promise to love not to harden our hearts
to promise too in our afterglow to come to know the other
with naked souls, again to vow in name and deed
the choice we make is given, not pleading
here and there as we go to call upon Him for His light of love
to strengthen each, not one or the other
together shared, the bond can't be broken.
Here in the shelter, under the glow of love
we whisper together touching each other's hearts.

It was in candle light
its strange wonderful glow
when first he felt her love envelope him so
there beneath the shadow eerie as it were
the whisper of her song came unto his ear.
Love was all about him to accept it as it is—
change not a note of love's music, it is very clear
golden trumpets pound his heart
an angel's drum beat brings in his day
to make good her acquaintance in the splendid light of May
to move among the lilies, to go gently through the field
to softly speak of love; her heart is there to steal.
Yet in a quiet moment gently in the field
so softly her song singing, patience he, to let her heart heal.

Sonnet 59

Take pity on a weary traveler
tend to me, fix me up, then pray for me
help me then, bring me to your sun
at night lean me up, point me in direction of the moon
share with me good fortune, glad tidings and the like
lie down beside me, wrap me in your smile
be with me in the morrow, take flight with me today
show me the proper way
to love you till all is Glory, 'till the ending of the day
when that night comes to me
and clouds, stars, moonlit sky do fade
you may take sweet delight in love you've created, made.
Let that be years from now, not now the time for woe
have pity on this weary traveler, first take me off the road.

Will I have strung strings to a heart
shared a love then quick like breath depart
like the bird of light on the wing always in flight
or cunning like an eager parasite?
Will I have seen the universe
intimately, known others and shared their space
and have loved the stars in God's galaxy
pondered the question why He made me, me?
The essence of my verse, will it touch another's soul
perhaps to heal, perhaps help make them whole
shall I be remembered for my verse
or the humanity that I disperse?
Look well and deep within my verse, will it speak of me
and in the finding of said verse, will it set me free?

Sonnet 61

O to think that never again shall I see
another pure heart such as thee
nor place my hand on thy breast
to feel pulsating blood within thy chest
nor hear the sweetest sounds of thy breath.
I'll pluck out mine eye so that my mind may see
to fashion a sculpture as I remember thee,
listen close to whispering green blades of grass
like the breath of yours that is of my past
and under the veil of night, dreams of thee I'll hold tight
For what is left for me: only the light of thee within dreams
no defense nor will to fight, love you've taken, stripped me of
might.

Let no man say I've forsaken thee
for rich are my dreams of thee and me.

Passion aflame, an itching desire
toward nothing more than a life together.
Love needs wit, truth, praise, and honor
eye to eye down to our souls, willing to abdicate control
to rainbows of light, ironies of life, bright sunflowers
vast fields of watercolors
to our wandering hands the silver moon for lovers
underneath the woolen gray old covers
nothing petty ever to last
to bend, not crack, in uncertain times remaining steadfast
'till the cool sea breeze of a gentle summer's wind
always be my lover, always be my friend.
Wretched is he that debates alone
no light in his life, his good counsel gone.

Sonnet 63

Not you but me when the heart it does deceive
itself, for want of a fulfilling need outside itself, it does perceive
every passing glance, an eye that glints—there lies true romance
not remembering to remember love is an amorphous thing
lacking form, it sometimes lies, sometimes stings.
Yet the heart does keep in store
that once it knew love, shared it long before
those not-forgotten days of seashore light, of spring and play
golden sand, sunny beach, wintry nights and log fire days.
Yesteryear is long time past, the pain gone but the memories last
to feed and sustain the soul, to keep the mind healthy and whole
to weather every painful fire lest the absence of love take its toll.
To you I thought to lend my heart, in you I thought to depend
ever circular the painful part when outside myself I went again.

Sonnet 64

O, that one thousand times I could stand before your eyes
one thousand times never be denied the beauty before my eye
one thousand times I'd love you in every way with each dawn
through the hours, through the passing of the day
one thousand times my prayers would search the skies
that safe would be your way, your path to be sublime
one thousand times my name you'd whisper in the night
when planets shift, the night grows white, stars burst after a time
one thousand times in every single day a vow to you to make:
no love will be truer than that I have for you, save one—the

Maker;

He alone I shall not outdo. He alone can love you more than I
but I'm His competition 'till the day I die.
One thousand times I'll repeat this simple prayer
"Oh Lord though she be yours, oh Lord can we share?"

Sonnet 65

How come I to this woeful plight—
to look upon thy face both day and night
to hear thy voice as it sings notes as soft
as valley winds and powder clouds that float aloft?
O thy perfume fills the air with wonderment—
such despair but my love for you is vehement
suffer you do not my incorrigible way
think you, it is a nuisance by night and day
some greater love has tempted thee
conspired to lift your love from me
say you a gentle lover of some youth
you've traded old for young and therein lies truth.
Not now will you I hate, nor be angry at the fates—
but old, ah there's a thing to hate, hate, and hate!

Sonnet 66

Tonight, again I drown in pools of blue
again in winter's scene I stand in front of you
with flakes falling big as summer birds in flight
you turn a wintry day into a summer's delight
a winter's scene that's cold, stark, and bare
a caustic chill over barren land fills the air
yet a light touch by you alleviates winter's despair.
Sunny's disposition is a wealth of light
where she walks winter's chill takes immediate flight
budding roses appear to grow up out of the melting snow
acute visions of sunflowers and a glorious golden meadow
and I again can look forward to tomorrow—
Winter is tragic, bleak, and dreary, with abundant shadows
yet it's a wondrous day when Sunny walks by my windows.

What's this thing that tames me, lays my soul bare
creeps through my innards—lays waste to me there?
What's this thing that wrests all control
leaves me atremble, manifests itself in a body whole?
What's this thing that changes night into day
pushes me down to a knee to the Lord to pray?
What's this thing all beauty and sublime?
Never have I known such beauty to my eye...
What's this thing that's all gentle and rare
to take a man of discontent and do a total repair?
What's this thing—someone give it a name—
why it enlivens the spirit, removes lingering pain.
What's this thing—can't you hear my cry?
But know you this: I want to keep it till the day I die.

Why then does my heart bleed
when love itself is all it needs?
Surely love brings not pain—
how then shall I have the will to gain
when my love has taken flight
in stealth left me in the pitch of night.
O that I should know where my love's flown—
how could I've prevented, how could I've known?
when like icy wind she blistered me
and in her I placed all that was best of me
and like wilted flower sapped of strength
life has lost its color and its nectar's spent.
Spring is with color blooming
will love come back again, gentle, unassuming?

Sonnet 69

Oh that I were he, head in your
lap—oh sweet luxury
to smell the nectar of your breath
to nuzzle these lips on your neck
to frolic with you in the pitch, 'till light
to lovingly hand over my heart
to swear alliance, we'd never part—
this hand would place on your fair skin
a potion so powerful you'd swear you'd sinned
for a love so cataclysmic has no earthly beginning
and like infinity surely would have no ending—
it's these lips moving but it's the soul that's speaking.
That a gift so precious would ever see me
honored I'd be, bright as fleur-de-lis.

And yet, earth sings your praise
without your walk the sky turns a murky haze
to you each feathered friend that flies
whistles to your ear a sweet lover's cry
and Nature's wondrous act of spring
puts roses in your cheeks, a sign of its blossoming.
Can it be that while you sleep
heavenly angels that watch around you weep
at the absence of their friend—
to know without your light, darkness has no end
while at your beck and call animal, bird, and plant
await your arrival to join you in spiritual covenant.
How important you must be to spring
that nothing lives until you sing.

I cannot praise you more than I do
and to myself remain honest and true
I cannot love you more than He
nor impeach His name to claim you, Hazel Lee
yet you are my life and indispensable to me.
Daily in the mirror I see
clearly the face of God in you and me
and a whisper of His name
where you are, so His glory so His fame.
If truth be guided by His light
then I'm to love you both day and night
if He knows not wrong then it must be right.
I cannot praise you more than I do;
if God is love then so must I love you.

When all is chronicled in the book of time
each word and verse scrutinized line by line
no time will be given to formulate a lie
no questions of morality will arise
but the quest for truth and love, was it satisfied?
from yourself you can not hide
do you expect to hide from the All-Seeing Eye?
the color of love leaves one color-blind
truth walks tall with a magnificent stride
and each man and woman given their own private test
for their road journeyed will be concave at best
a route pock-marked and riddled with lust.
A journey taken in the dead pitch of night
shouldn't have an itinerary that's outside the Light.

Sonnet 73

Children, oh children, that I could tell you
the world is just a fine place, you'd never be blue
that carousels, spinning tops are fresh painted and new
that lies are outdated and fallacy a naked ploy
good comes out of evil for young girls and boys;
children, oh children, I shall not lie to you
the world can be unfair, unkind, speak dark untruths
yet you needn't be afraid, you needn't hide your heads
believe in your Angels, they'll keep you in good stead
they'll walk with you in the day, stay with you at night
if you ask them nice they'll lead you to do what's right
Angels are close to God and understand His might;
Children, oh children, to be kind and fair
is never quite easy, but is Godly, precious, and dear.

It's not a faint, vain, amorphous thing—
torment numbs, resounds, and loudly rings—
it laughs while it shreds a heart
bleeds you dry while you're being torn apart
it's cruel and without a care
watches you drown in your own despair
aches in places you've never felt pain
screams in the night wondering what's the gain
reeks of death and yet it never comes
a nightmare in daylight with ungodly rhythms
it plagues the brain, burns and seethes
a minute, a second, you plead for relief.
Such is the nature of unrequited love
whom is to blame but only He above.

Sonnet 75

That I should no longer wander aimless
or never again know the absence of bliss
that my passion is aroused at last to come to this;
my fire burning, so evenly stoked a love given
not wasted as smoke, but pleasurably driven;
for that end I thank the gods that command the heavens
yet I wonder for all my well-traveled years
where she was, did she know fears?
did she think I would not arrive, wonder at the delay?
for the rest of my life I shall apologize each day
I will whisper in her hear words to calm her fears
and never again will there be a need for tears.
The road was well-traveled though I was alone
but each minute gone was a minute I wanted home.

Sonnet 76

Where does it go this light I need
that illumines my eye kindles my heart?
Does it fracture into specks of bright
ounces of gold dust of prism parts
filling others' lifeblood with richness
yet filling my cup with abundant emptiness
where this light indeed? Born once to me unselfishly
which I supped upon most greedily
never thinking it to end with inflamed hostility
it claims from me no animosity
but wanting to understand this adversity
kills me by degrees;
That my guiding light shines not on me
shall I then love the warmth of autumn or its breeze?

It has come now, silent in the warm
gentle sun it waits to be born
into its infinite wisdom
beyond what is known
precise in its place, doing no harm
its procreation necessary, hopes for the common:
like helium light it will give songs to hum
lifting the spirits of the unloved and downtrodden
to be whispered sweetly from the lips of a mom
to endorse what is right for the ex-wife on her own
to take out of a life for a moment the gale of maelstrom
to float in the air full of life when full grown;
The word that gives the color of light
the word that brightens the darkest night.

Sonnet 78

You bid me adieu then I say fair
with it say goodbye to dark brown hair
and to the eyes that fire the mid-night air;
then I say wait, lest you speed off in haste and bad cheer
and stiff as frost biting in the mid-winter clear.
Yes I've erred, cheated, a false face masqueraded
laid at your feet lies and dishonor
with naught to acquit myself but much loss to ponder;
can I not earn back my honor, to flower again like a rose of

summer

bring back to you me, your inferior former lover?
Bid me adieu, I say fair but bitter it is to be beyond repair—
fault's but my own to hear you say "wait a year."
The lesson here for those who tinker
chase the skirt you shall not be a victor.

Dark the cobbled streets where lonely shuffling feet
move in solitude with a heart that's beat and bruised
in the stench and unclean air life has come to this unfair
The weight of all the woe has killed half the spirit attacked the soul
the black reaper is here to claim what's left of the Flame
the reaper gladly shares the pain in the dark and ugly rain;
no the Flame it won't go nor give in to the woe:
for on the morrow there might be fresh and bright clean air
or clear pure rain to wash away both the filth and the pain
a bright bouquet of the sun to put a life where there was none
and the warmth of its gold to make the soul whole again
no the reaper he won't claim it, not today not the Flame;
One night's poison surreal hear the ring of life's death knell
morning brings the sun casts a spell and all is well all is well.

None but you knew the pain the woe
to none but you did the pain I show:
Know you a thousand nights I'd walked the street
a thousand times known my life was incomplete
a thousand times seen you reflected in the glass
a thousand times heard whispers from said glass
on a lampless street but never had the nerve to ask
why it haunts me with my past; how dull the glass
that reflects back to me an empty face pale and weak
shoulders hunched, lifeless eyes that no longer seek
dull flowers in need of weeding
in need of help before they die;
So sweet a love in you once grew
every day was a wonder—bright, glorious, and new.

Sonnet 81

It's only my dark eyes and heart that hurt
unjustly skirted then flagrantly deserted
by her that was my Muse and sage in better days
with loving thoughts and grand designs of which now I'm
deprived;
she no longer warms my heart with her heated touch
nor fills my eyes with her olive skin.
Like the wanting of the sun that's longed for much
in a season of rain, I'm begging and pleading to let love begin
love removed from me the sweetest fruit of any tree
in the Garden of Eden where life had its golden origin
plucked away from my grasp now it's death by degrees
it's only my dark eyes and heart that hurt me;
Oh when shall seasons begin when love is fair without end
the sun warms lovers' hearts and each to the other is friend.

Sonnet 82

Oh woe I swear the pain drifts through the air
it clings to you and me, it tears a heart like a bell it rings
it shouts, it yells, it's never quiet and always tells
both friend and foe alas it wants all to know
it's there both day and night, it's never ever far from sight
it's woe-begotten, never gone, it lingers like an ill-writ song
it dances prances in a midnight clear, laughs loudly seeing tears
when you're up it pushes down, it never smiles, only frowns;
some say it hates the sun, alas so wrong that's where it has its fun
to see a face in a looking glass, pain worn like a masquerade mask
high on a balcony pain awaits, drifts down to give others grief;
But here's a trick or two to keep dreaded pain away from you
love strong stayed wrapped in a lover's arms, remember youth.

Sonnet 83

Ah dear lady, you with sharp mind, black tresses
quick wit, you set about to deceive and pretend
yet your words give you away
methinks you come from nobler stock
ornaments of charm and guile
those that think otherwise should keep a sharp eye out
lest they be ensnared in your false subtleties
you my beauty shall not play that trick on me
you my beauty with understated smile
an eye that sees more than others see
you my beauty shan't play that trick on me
for I am already bewitched by thy smile;
Fools fools oh the poor fools
they know not that the woman rules!

Sonnet 84

I am old without spring in my heart
I am old but not without fire
within the veins that boil lust desire
I don't wallow but sinisterly conspire
to liven the night with wanton schemes
that plague me through venal dreams
which in daylight are clearly seen
my mirror reflects back that which is obscene
youth is vanished and age has conquered me
and more's the pity, for these eyes still see
the wonders of the heavens the glory of the seas
the color of romance in her eyes and cheeks;
Spring, Spring come back fill my heart
though my youth is gone you need not depart.

Sonnet 85

Give no weight to what I say
I say I love you best now and can no more
beyond all good sense adore you;
like the rose which has yet to full bloom
is not the rose still a beauty in spring?
the diamond in the rough
still a diamond? a bit of polish heightens its cost;
then my love is at its best today
when comes the morrow brighter then
and brighter still when comes another day
yet in the moon's blue-gray light
the power of your love which brings my heart to flight;
The weight of my love is beyond kept score
with each day that passes I love you more.

Sonnet 86

I will start this sonnet from the middle
for there is fear in its ending
for the sonnet has no friend
and its loneliness is pending
there is comfort in the middle
that's where brightness lays
words that surround it are clever inlays
like being deep in a belly safe and warm
there's comfort in the middle far from storms
like being wrapped in a sheepskin blanket
or held secure in your arms
there's comfort in the middle far from tempestuous longings;
And of the beginning there is much to dread
the distance to the middle is like being unfed.

Sonnet 87

(for B)

Never did he know
the letting go would hurt so
like the tempest wind blowing outside the window
whipping the leaves baring the trees
oh, the letting go
of the beauty of the glory days of spring
lavender-colored days that let the heart sing
oh, the letting go
closing the heart's window
shedding the pain, letting go
and yet, his love soars...lingers in the air
like the sun forever...pleading for repair;
Thinking of you brings
his mind to flight without wings.

Sonnet 88

Farewell my heart, farewell
you've taken flight, farewell;
farewell rest-filled nights and peaceful dreams
innocence is lost, days now filled with wonder
love is all that it seemed, she now fills my dreams
farewell to gloomy nights and rainy days
ice-cold heart and muddled thought
she's my sun she is my shade in all ways
my highest mountain to attain
cools my brow like emerald lakes
wherever she wanders near or far
my heart she takes;
Fare thee well my heart, fare thee well
where she is you sit well, farewell my heart farewell.

Sonnet 89

Let this be the last thing I write
as I take this journey—or is it flight —
through Brussels where I held my breath
in Copenhagen where the blues came to rest
in Holland where I saw only night
saw your eyes absent of their light
in Germany when crossing the strait
pain flew down, the body ached
felt it in blues and reds a heavy weight
in France you stood idly by while my cloud burst
but your well is dry so I suffer with the hurt
I remember the silence in front of an English hearth;
This will be the last thing I write
love ran off in the pale moonlight.

Sonnet 90

How does the wind blow, smooth or rough?
When will you let me know?
You are afraid of me, my eyes tell your future, they see;
What is it you've come to know, will we be in a room alone
will I lay on your breast, there to come to nest?
Tell me what it is you think;
I am here with thirst and need to drink
of love of life and warmth of you to alleviate all my blues
to hear you shout my name your center is my want my gain
my summer my spring your soul and heart in my ear singing
words loudly ringing rushing forth like a waterfall
like pure rain quenching the earth and all
I will come know you your center your all in all;
How does the wind blow?
wait I for my love to let me know.

What can be failure if her love has yet to unfold?
Winter can be long and the rose remains closed
till spring comes bursting with sunshine and dew
water fresh for the earth to renew
and skies bright as diamonds of an unparalleled hue.
What can be failure if her arms remain closed?
Spring has promised that nothing remains glued
spring brings on summer and a wondrous life's view
of merriment that winter never knew
failure is brief and awkward and blue
like winter cold and unfeeling too;
Though she's cold to me on this blustery night
await I for summer to share in her sweet delight.

Sonnet 92

Had I been a soothsayer
I would have forewarned myself
armed myself against such an invasion
taken higher ground, closed my ear to your persuasion
taken the offensive not defended against what was given
the warning, the sound of the alarm was unheeded
the attack swift and never impeded
and my one magnificent jewel lost forever
you were smart beautiful and clever
with your guile you could reshape the heavens
the gods would say it was their pleasure
for you are a woman beyond all measure;
Ah, such a sweet attack
alas, for me there's no turning back.

Sonnet 93

In idle moments they bloom and grow, the flowers
whether dry or moist, in or out of doors they grow
in patch-worked fields or barren soil they grow the flowers
in the darkest night even in the salty air they grow
the driest weeds or reddest rose they grow the flowers
in shade in the sun in humidity where there's none they grow
spring, winter, summer, fall, some are short others tall
some spiral high up in the air, others with an inch to spare but

grow

some live long, while others die but all bring beauty to the eye
some need water, others don't care, others a touch, others air to

grow

purple petals, green bulbs, a black orchid, pansies
flowers by the asphalt road they grow;
How like love the flowers
touch air and care to grow.

Sonnet 94

When I think of you, comes the sonnet
slow though not as an opponent
snail-like laborious with love and good intent
heart open and the merging imminent
full of love's wonder with you the recipient
and I equal to the task a slave and subservient
mixing words, superlatives, finding their proper ingredients:
nouns, pronouns, verbs, and adjectives past and present
words that linger, smolder, words that ignite like flint
words that baffle, struggle, words that are recalcitrant
words that praise and sing, words with wings that lift
words that dance on strings like a puppet or a marionette;
When I think of you comes the sonnet
laboriously, lovingly, with good intent I and the words are spent.

You light up life with resplendent beauty
you walk the earth, it's been adjudged your duty
from state to state or commonwealth
the brilliance of your smile brings good health
where you plant your feet shade is born
so a tree, so lotus blossoms, so the sun
so are born fairies everywhere
to put the joy of love in the air
where there's the lightness of your touch
a cool spring breeze on a hot summer's day it means much
where you place your honey-lipped kiss
if thundering rain, turns to a gentle calming mist;
Perhaps you think I've overstated
nothing said will be taken back or negated.

Sonnet 96

Your touch forever marks a man
like some ancient tattoo—its branding
sure as the Ancients painted the cave
your brand marks the skin to forever stay
and though many a year goes by
your brand will stay clear to the eye
like a shelter where a man may go
when his life is empty and full of woe
yes the shelter of your brand
when your touch once marked him a man
in colors magnificent to the eye
when together love was riding high;
And yet though your love has long ago flown
your brand is clear to remain life-long.

Sonnet 97

Come catch a brilliant star with me
ride the red-hot nova and let's be
starlight in each others eyes
a starburst inundating the massive sky
conjoined stardust fleeting by
or swoosh across in the pale moonlight
be blown apart like heavy particles of dust
by the tail of a dazzling comet of love
carried in space on the wings of a dove
let's flame up in the darkest hour of night
leaving love trails as we alight;
And each time we set to flame
the world is ours, love too is our gain.

Undone! That I am undone
my penance has yet to come
ambling lost, ashamed I am undone
remorse weighs heavy on my soul
without your light I've no control
blemished, tarnished, bereft of goal
to wander aimless alone
your love was my wealth, my gold
the guiding hand that kept me whole
you were the epic riches I let go
before me is nothing but silent woe;
Though my treasure chest is depleted
my spirit is weak but not defeated.

In the blueness of the night
is when the music hurts
it wraps itself around the heart
tightens, makes blood come in spurts
it clings to you in mid-night
like the shadows on the walls
you lie in bed wondering will daylight
come at all; and that would be a plus
for music in daylight lightens up a heart
ceases to weep and wail remembers
those darkened hours and fly-by-night
lovers that once played upon your fears;
Dark may be the blues that wail through the night
but morning birds and dew the music that puts blues to flight.

Wait for me on your next page of life
where the sun forever glistens in your eye
wait for me as you turn the page
moving as you will into another stage
wait for me, don't leave me behind
the struggle is hard, I'll make that climb
wait for me, I'll not show fear
I'll share your vision though my own is unclear
wait for me though I'm not as bright as you
I've enough character to see it through
wait for me along the border's edge
it's there that I will take the pledge;
In all that you ever thought or dreamed to do
God as my witness I'll be there to support you.

My eyes tire—the weeping the tears
the heart pumps alone with its fears
all its emotions crest as waves for years
love known belongs to my yesteryears
now and then your shadow reappears
night moon bright cloud cover disappears
what's left is the silence awful silence and tears
they've burdened my shoulders for untold years
but long I do for my yesteryears
when the shadow of my youth she reappears
then for the moment all my fears disappear;
Then there in the half moon light
love returns my heart's alight.

Other books by
Clyde A. Wray

CAUSE EVERYBODY AIN'T A HERO
ISBN 0-9659811-0-X

SONNETS FOR LOVERS & STRANGERS
ISBN 0-9659811-1-8

Published by Poetry For Your Ear Publishing
5259 North Sepulveda Boulevard
Suite 18
Sherman Oaks, CA 91411